My First BIG Book of SPACE FACTS

by Ruth Owen

Ruby Tuesday Books

Published in 2022 by Ruby Tuesday Books Ltd.

Designer: Emma Randall
Editor: Mark J. Sachner
Production: John Lingham

Photo credits:
Creative Commons: 17 bottom; ESA: 42 top; ESA/ Hubble: 40; ESO: 52–53; NASA: 27, 30–31, 33, 34–35, 36–37, 38–39, 39 top, 47, 50–51, 53 bottom, 54 top, 59, 62–63, 64–65, 70–71, 80–81, 82–83, 84–85, 86–87; Public Domain: 31 bottom, 32 top, 41, 42 bottom, 48 top, 49 top; Ruby Tuesday Books: 18 bottom, 19, 20–21, 23, 56 top, 75; Shutterstock: Cover, 1, 2–3, 5 top, 5 bottom (Denis Belitsky), 6 (Arena Creative), 7 (mikolajn), 8 (Stock-Asso), 9 (Zakharchuk), 10 (Jacek Fulawka), 11 top (Dmitry Rukhlenko), 11 bottom (Anton Balazh), 12–13, 14–15 (Muratart), 15 top left (fizkes), 15 top right (Ljubomir Trigubishyn), 16 (Lia Koltyrina), 17 top, 18 top, 22, 24, 25 (alexaldo), 26 (Jurik Peter), 26 bottom (voyager624), 28–29, 29 bottom (Terrance Emerson), 30 (Pike-28), 43, 44–45, 46, 48–49 (Canadastock), 54 bottom, 55, 56 bottom, 57, 58 top (Siberian Art), 58 bottom (Elena11), 60, 61 (Catmando), 66–67 (Marcos Silva), 68 top, 68 bottom (Warachai Krengwirat), 70–71, 72–73, 76, 77 top Galyna Andrushko, 77 bottom (DenVDen), 78 (Kit Leong), 79 top, 79 bottom (Gorodenkoff), 88 top (GreSiStudio), 88 bottom (Robsonphoto), 89 top (Shelley Dark), 89 bottom (Rido/Asaf Weizman/ Sofiaworld/cbpix/Albert Beukhof), 90–91, 92–93 (Angela Harburn/Roman 3D Art/egg design/DM7); Shutterstock (IgorZH): 69, 74–75.

Library of Congress Control Number: 2021919968
Print (hardback) ISBN 978-1-78856-250-8
Print (paperback) ISBN 978-1-78856-251-5
eBook PDF ISBN 978-1-78856-252-2
ePub ISBN 978-1-78856-253-9

Published in Minneapolis, MN, United States

www.rubytuesdaybooks.com

What's Inside?

What Is Outer Space?

When you look up at the **stars** in the black night sky, that is outer space.

Out in space there are

MILLIONS AND MILLIONS AND MILLIONS AND MILLIONS AND MILLIONS AND MILLIONS OF BRIGHT STARS!

Space and everything in it is called the universe.

In space there are also **planets**, **moons**, **comets**, and big space rocks called **asteroids**.

A comet

Stars still shine brightly during the day. We just can't see them because of the Sun's bright light.

Stars

What Is a Star?

Twinkle twinkle little star. . . .
A star might look little, but that's just
because it's a long way away.

A star is a giant ball of gases.

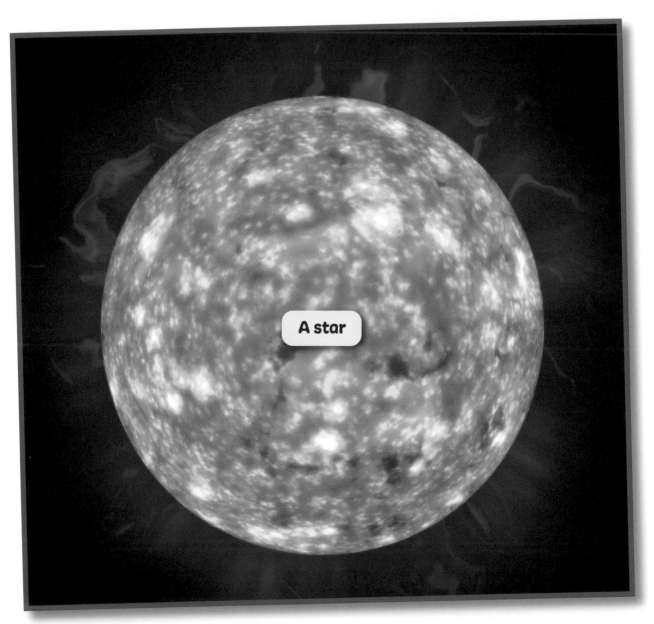

A star

As the gases burn, they make heat and light.

This is a **HUGE** cloud of gas and dust in outer space.

It is called a **nebula**.

Inside a nebula, the gases form into new stars.

A nebula

A nebula is like a star factory!

How Many Stars Are in Space?

If we look through a telescope, we can see millions of stars.

But even the biggest, most powerful telescope can't see the whole universe.

Can we figure out how many stars there are?

Some scientists tried to answer the question using math.

They think there could be

one thousand trillion

stars in the universe!

That giant number looks like this:

1,000,000,000,000,000,000,000

That's more stars than there are grains of sand on Earth!

What Is the Sun?

The Sun is actually a star. Our star!

It looks much bigger in the sky than all the other stars.

That's because it's the closest star to Earth.

Earth

BE SUN SAFE!
You should NEVER look straight at the Sun even if you are wearing sunglasses.

Looking at the Sun will badly damage your eyes.

Just like other stars, the Sun makes heat and light.

If we didn't have the Sun's heat and light, our planet would be a dark, frozen lump of ice-covered rock!

Frozen Earth

No people, animals, or plants could live on Earth if there was no Sun.

How Big Is the Sun?

If we compare the Sun to planet Earth,
it is big. Very big!

The Sun

Earth

The Sun measures about 865,000 miles (1.4 million km) across.

That's as wide as 110 Earths, side by side.

Space scientists use special equipment and spacecraft to take photos of the Sun, like this one.

This means we can all safely look at pictures of our amazing star.

How Far Away Is the Sun?

Earth is about 93 million miles (150 million km) from the Sun.

That's a long, long way, but it's just the right distance for our planet.

If we were closer to the Sun, Earth would get too hot.

Then all the water would dry up.

If Earth were farther from the Sun, it would be so cold that all the water would freeze.

People, animals, and plants need water to live.

Is Our Sun the Biggest Star?

Space scientists called **astronomers** compare the sizes of different stars. Our Sun is a medium-sized star.

The Sun

Earth

This is a giant loop of super-hot gas.

Some stars in the universe are smaller than the Sun.

But other stars are much, much bigger!

A star called Antares is hundreds of times bigger than the Sun.

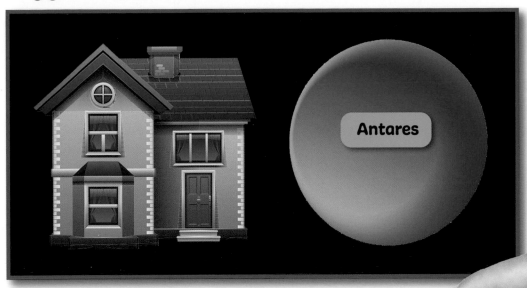

Antares

If Antares was the size of a house, our Sun would only be the size of a pea!

Pea-sized Sun

Antares

Where Does the Sun Go at Night?

Every evening, the Sun sets and then disappears from the sky. Why?

Setting Sun

Earth

Our Earth is rotating, or spinning, like a top.

When the place where you live faces towards the Sun, it is daytime for you.

Daytime

Nighttime

Then the place where you live spins away from the Sun's light and it gets dark.

The Sun is still there, but now it's nighttime for you.

In real life, Earth and the Sun are not this close.

What Is a Planet?

A planet is a large, round object in space.

A planet travels, or
orbits, around and
around a star.

Earth

Our Earth is a planet. It is
orbiting our star, the Sun.

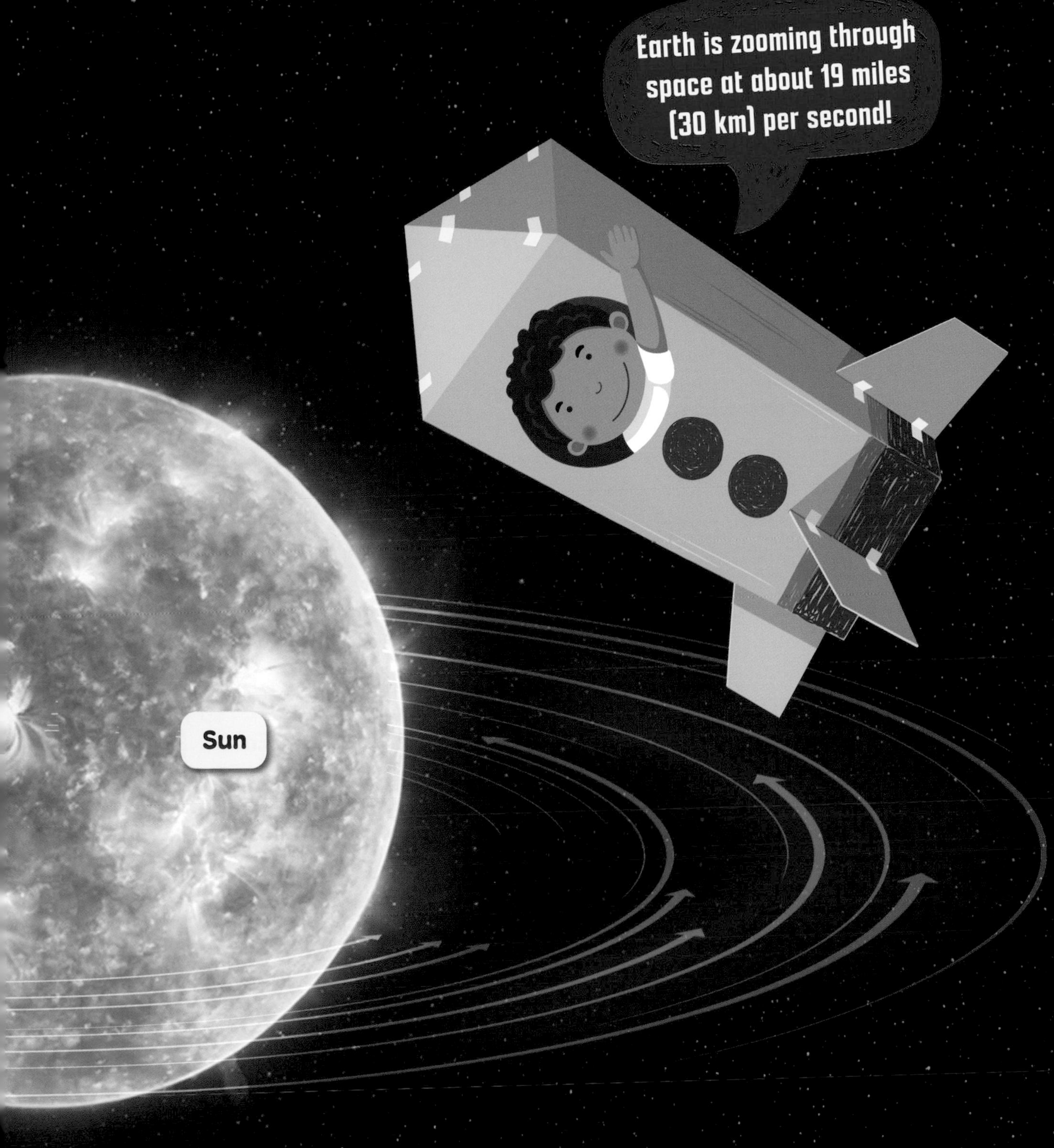

It takes 365 days for Earth to orbit the Sun once. We call this time a year.

What Is the Solar System?

Earth has lots of space neighbors.

There are seven other planets
traveling around the Sun.

Mercury

Venus

Earth

Mars

Jupiter

Saturn

Uranus

Neptune

The planets all
look very different.

Small planets called **dwarf planets** also orbit the Sun.
So do rocky asteroids and icy comets.

Uranus

Neptune

Pluto is a dwarf planet.

Mars

Jupiter

Mercury

Comet

Sun

Earth

Pluto

Venus

Asteroids

Saturn

The Sun and all these space objects are
called the **solar system**.

How Big Are the Solar System Planets?

**Some of the planets in the
solar system are smaller than Earth.**

Earth

Mercury

Mercury is the
smallest planet in
the solar system.

Others are much, much bigger.

Jupiter is as wide as
11 planet Earths!

It's the biggest planet
in the solar system.

Jupiter

Earth

This picture shows the planets compared to each other and the Sun.

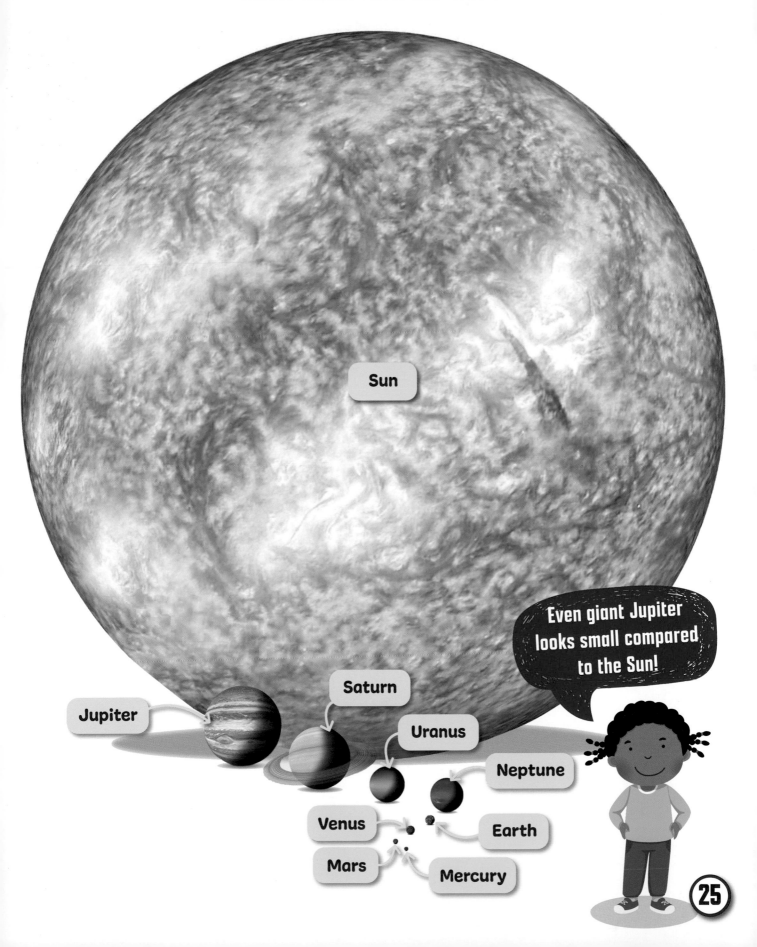

What Is It Like on Mercury?

Mercury is the closest planet to the Sun.

In the daytime, it's 10 times hotter on Mercury than on Earth.

A metal spacecraft might melt if it landed on this planet!

Lots of asteroids and comets hit Mercury.

They make big holes called **craters**.

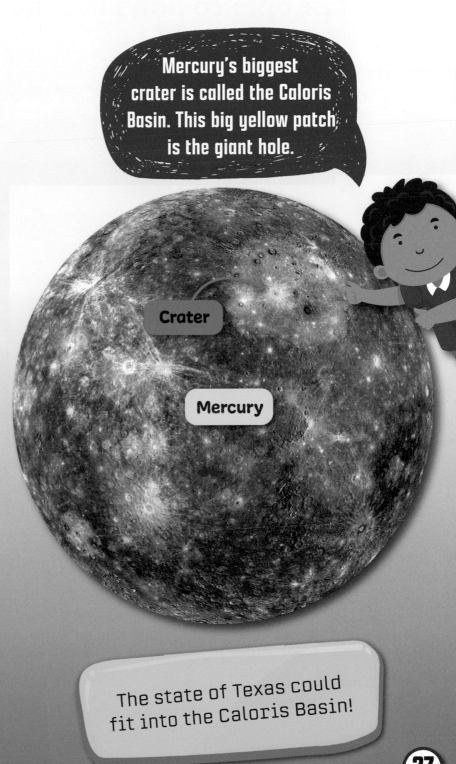

Mercury's biggest crater is called the Caloris Basin. This big yellow patch is the giant hole.

Crater

Mercury

The state of Texas could fit into the Caloris Basin!

Could We Live on Venus?

Venus is the closest planet to Earth, but people couldn't live there.

Venus

On Venus it is super-hot and the air is poisonous.

This picture shows how Venus has thick clouds that block out the Sun's light.

Even in daytime it is dark there.

Venus has more than 1,000 volcanoes.

Moon

Sometimes we can see Venus shining in the sky.

Venus looks bright because the Sun's light makes the planet's clouds shine.

What Is It Like on Mars?

On Mars, it is colder than inside a freezer!

North Pole

Mars

Just like Earth, Mars has an icy North Pole.

The land is covered with rocks and reddish-brown, dusty soil.

Strong winds blow dust up into the air.

This makes the sky on Mars look pinkish-brown.

Sky filled with dust

Mountain

Sometimes, Mars is completely covered with one giant dust storm.

Dusty soil

Mars is much smaller than our home planet, Earth.

Earth

Mars

Which Planet Has the Tallest Mountain?

The tallest mountain on Earth is Mount Everest.
It is about 5.5 miles (9 km) high, but it's
not the biggest mountain in the solar system.

Mount Everest

Mars has an even
bigger mountain called
Olympus Mons.

Olympus Mons

Everest

Let's say it!
oh-LIM-pus MAHNS

If Olympus Mons was put on Earth, it would almost cover the whole of France!

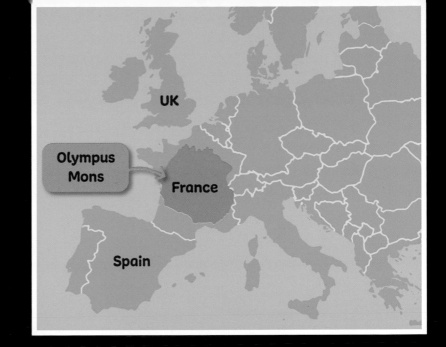

UK

Olympus Mons

France

Spain

Olympus Mons

Olympus Mons is actually a volcano. It is almost 14 miles (22 km) high!

Are There Robots on Mars?

Yes! Space scientists on Earth send robot rovers to explore Mars.

Robot Name	Landed on Mars
Sojourner	1997
Spirit	2004
Opportunity	2004

Robot Name	Landed on Mars
Curiosity	2012
Perseverance	2021
Zhurong	2021

The robots have wheels and can drive over the rocky land.

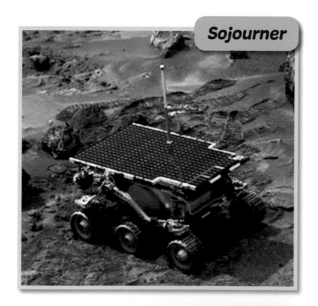

Sojourner

Opportunity

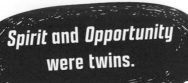

Spirit and *Opportunity* were twins.

The rovers beam photos and information about Mars back to Earth.

Curiosity is the size of a big car. It takes selfies and sends them back to Earth!

Curiosity on Mars

Sojourner, *Spirit*, and *Opportunity* have now stopped working, but they are still on Mars.

What Will Perseverance the Robot Do?

Perseverance the robot rover blasted off to Mars in 2020.

Perseverance has lots of science tools on board. Why?

Scientists think that tiny living things called **microbes** once lived on Mars.

Perseverance is in here

Microbes

Perseverance is looking for clues that show this is true.

Perseverance

Perseverance carried a tiny helicopter called *Ingenuity* to Mars.

Ingenuity

Ingenuity is the first craft to ever fly on another planet!

Will Astronauts Visit Mars?

Yes! One day they will. The trip will take about nine months.

On Mars, the air is poisonous to humans.

The astronauts will build a special camp to live in. If they go outside, they will wear spacesuits.

Mars buggy

Mars camp

Astronaut

There are no rivers or lakes on Mars, but there is ice. Astronauts will melt ice to make water.

The astronauts will grow fruit and vegetables to eat inside their camp.

Would you like to visit Mars and become a Martian?

What Is Jupiter's Great Red Spot?

Jupiter is hundreds of millions of miles from Earth.

Jupiter

Great Red Spot

Thick clouds

On Jupiter, there are strong winds, fierce storms, and hurricanes.

Great Red Spot

Earth

One of the hurricanes looks like a giant reddish-orange circle. It is called the Great Red Spot.

This picture shows the size of Earth compared to the Great Red Spot.

A hurricane is a huge storm with powerful winds. The swirling winds circle around and around.

Which Planet Has Rings?

If you look at Saturn through a telescope, you will see it has rings.

Saturn

Rings

The rings are made of billions of pieces of ice and dust.

Saturn

Earth

This picture shows the size of Earth compared to Saturn.

Some of the pieces of ice and dust are as small as grains of sand.

Others are the size of a house.

Some pieces are as big as a mountain!

Which Planet Spins on Its Side?

As planets orbit the Sun, they also spin around.

Jupiter

Most planets spin in an upright position.

But Uranus spins on its side.

Uranus also spins in the opposite direction of most planets.

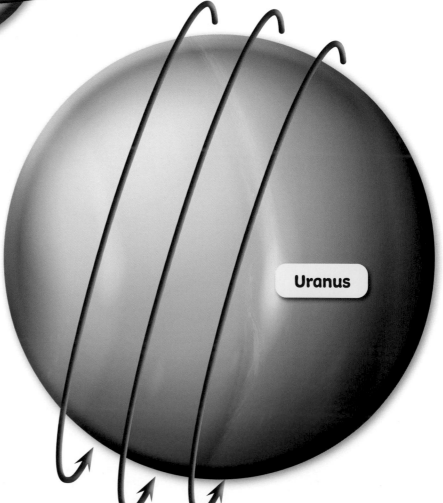

Uranus

Scientists think Uranus was once upright.

Then it was hit by another giant space object that knocked it onto its side!

Earth

Uranus

Uranus is four times wider than Earth.

Which Planet Has Diamond Rain?

On Neptune, gases in the air turn into diamonds.

Then the diamonds fall onto the planet like diamond rain!

There are storms on Neptune with super-fast winds. The winds blow at 1,500 miles (2,400 km) per hour.

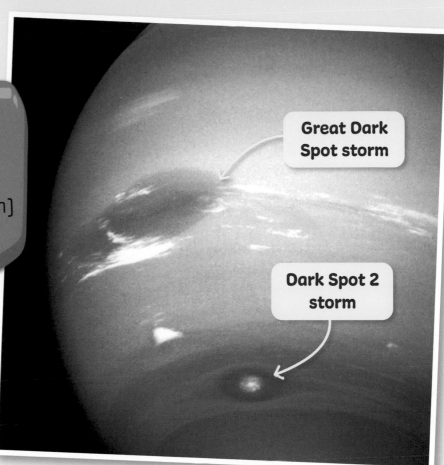

Great Dark Spot storm

Dark Spot 2 storm

Earth

Neptune

Earth takes just 365 days to travel around the Sun once.

Neptune is so far from the Sun, it takes almost 165 years!

Neptune is much bigger than Earth.

Rocky or Gassy?

Some planets are rocky. The others are gassy.

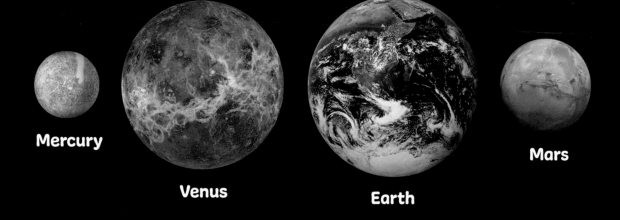

Mercury, Venus, Earth, and Mars
are solid planets made of rock.

Mercury

Venus

Earth

Mars

The outside of a rocky planet is called the crust.

It's easy to see Earth's rocky crust at the Grand Canyon in Arizona.

Jupiter, Saturn, Uranus, and Neptune are not solid.

They are called the **gas giants**.

Jupiter

Saturn

Uranus

Neptune

They are made of gases and liquids.

A spacecraft couldn't land on the gas giants.

A dwarf planet is a small, round space object.

Dwarf planets are much smaller than big planets like Earth and Mars.

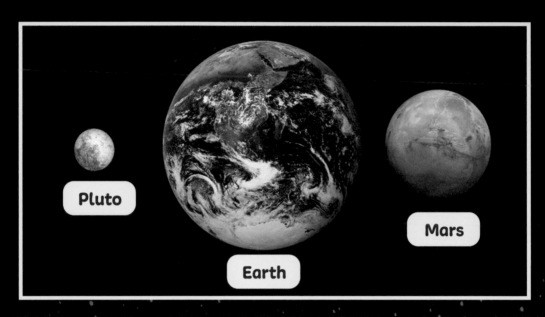

Pluto

Earth

Mars

Pluto is a
dwarf planet.

Pluto
(PLOO-toh)

So far, astronomers have found five dwarf planets traveling around the Sun.

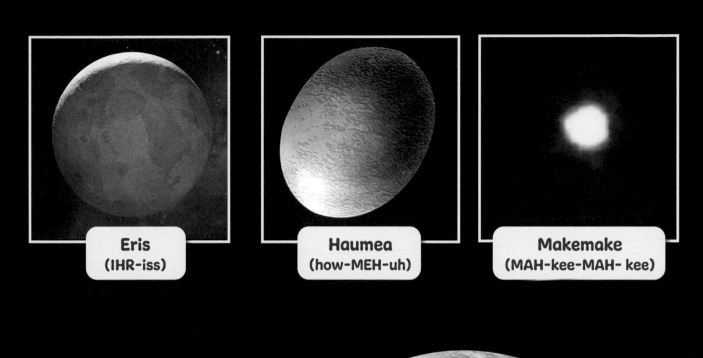

Eris
(IHR-iss)

Haumea
(how-MEH-uh)

Makemake
(MAH-kee-MAH- kee)

Ceres
(SIHR-eez)

Earth

This picture shows the size of Ceres compared to Earth.

Space scientists say that Ceres is a dwarf planet and an asteroid.

What Is It Like on Little Pluto?

The land on Pluto is icy and rocky.

It is colder than the coldest place on Earth.

Pluto is billions of miles from Earth and the Sun.

Pluto's surface

If you could stand on Pluto, the Sun would look like a tiny shining dot.

The Sun

Our home planet, Earth, has one Moon.

Little Pluto has five moons!

Charon

This is Pluto's biggest moon, Charon.

What Is the Moon?

The Moon is Earth's closest space neighbor.

Earth

The Moon

It is much smaller than the Earth.

As it gets dark at night, we see the Moon appear in the sky.

The Moon looks bright, but it doesn't make light.

The Sun shines on the Moon and lights it up.

That's why it looks so bright in the dark night sky.

The Moon is 238,900 miles (384,400 km) from Earth.

Why Does the Moon Change Shape?

The Moon is traveling, or orbiting, around and around Earth.

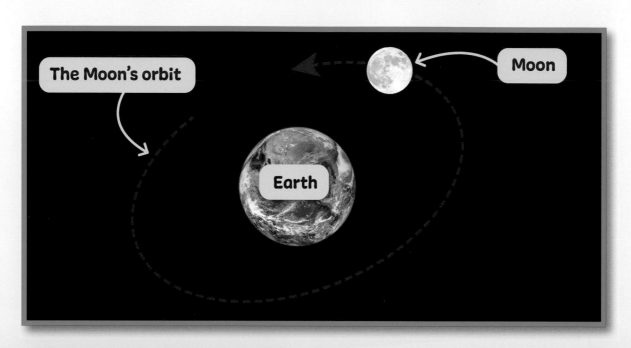

The Moon's orbit

Moon

Earth

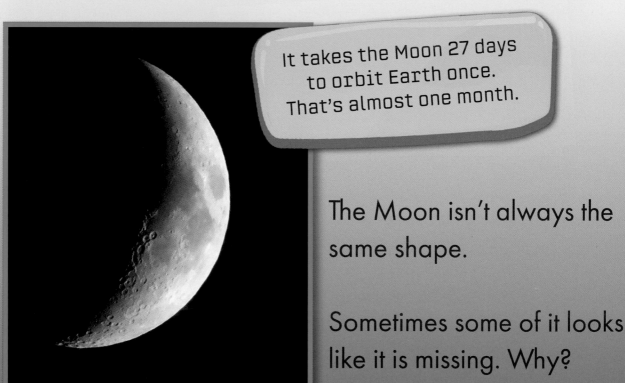

It takes the Moon 27 days to orbit Earth once. That's almost one month.

The Moon isn't always the same shape.

Sometimes some of it looks like it is missing. Why?

As the Moon travels around Earth each
month, we can't always see all of it.

Part of the
Moon we can see

Earth

Part of the
Moon we can see

We just see different parts of the Moon
shining in the night sky.

What Is the Moon Made of?

The Moon is mostly made of rock.
In its middle, there is a ball of iron.

Ball of iron

On the Moon, the ground is covered with rocks and thick, gray dust.

Moon dust

Astronaut footprints

This is what Earth looks like from the Moon.

On the Moon, the sky is black at night and in the daytime.

Moon rock

Astronaut on the Moon

Some rocks on the Moon are as big as trucks.

Moon buggy

Where Did the Moon Come From?

No one knows for sure.
But some scientists have an idea.

They think the Moon was made billions of years ago.

One day, a giant rocky space object hit Earth.

The object may have been another planet.

Chunks of rock flew out into space.

Then the rocks swirled around and around.

They clumped together and made the Moon!

What's on the Moon?

Long ago, people looked at the Moon through telescopes.

They saw dark patches that they thought were oceans.

Smooth, dark rock

Craters

Now we know these places are smooth, dark rock—not water!

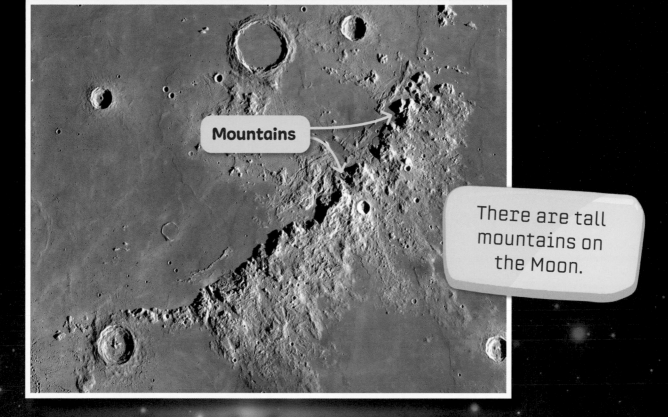

Mountains

There are tall mountains on the Moon.

There are thousands of craters on the Moon.

The Moon's South Pole

The biggest crater is 1,600 miles (2,600 km) across and 8 miles (13 km) deep.

Craters

The craters are made by asteroids and comets hitting the Moon.

Who Were the First People to Walk on the Moon?

In 1969, three astronauts went to the Moon.

Neil Armstrong

Michael Collins

Buzz Aldrin

This is *Columbia*.

Their spacecraft had different sections.

They sat in a tiny section called *Columbia*.

Neil and Buzz landed on the Moon
in a section called the *Eagle*.

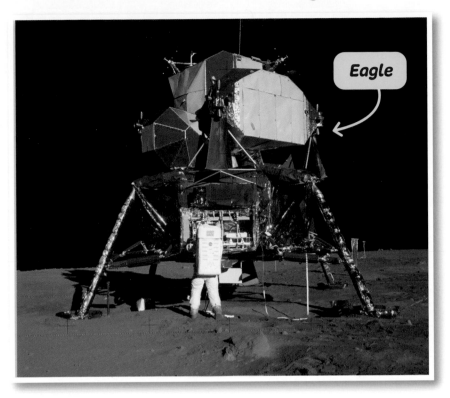

Eagle

They were the first people to ever
walk on the Moon.

Neil took this
photo of Buzz.
Can you spot Neil?

In total, 12 astronauts
have walked on the Moon.

Could People Live on the Moon?

Yes! Astronauts could build a special Moon base, or camp, to live in.

On the Moon, there is no air to breathe.

It is super-hot in the day.
At night it is colder than any place on Earth.

The base will protect the astronauts
and give them air.

Scientists think there is ice inside some Moon craters. The ice could be melted to make drinking water.

If they go outside, astronauts will wear spacesuits.

What Is an Eclipse?

**The Earth is traveling around the Sun.
And the Moon is traveling around the Earth.**

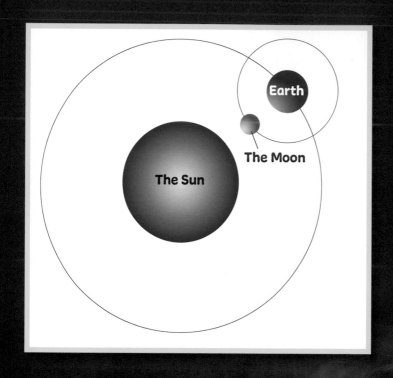

Sometimes, the Moon is between the Earth and the Sun in just the right position.

Then, an **eclipse** happens.

BE SUN SAFE!
Remember. NEVER look at the Sun.

The Moon

The Sun

Sometimes, the Moon blocks all the light from the Sun.

It may actually get dark for a few minutes—even though it's daytime!

This is called a total eclipse.

Is Our Moon the Only One?

No! There are lots and lots
of moons in the solar system.

How many moons?

Mercury
No moons

Venus
No moons

Earth
1 moon

Mars
2 moons

Jupiter—79 moons
(there may be more)

Saturn—82 moons
(there may be more)

Uranus—27 moons
(there may be more)

Neptune—14 moons
(there may be more)

Jupiter has a moon called Ganymede.

It is the biggest moon in the solar system.

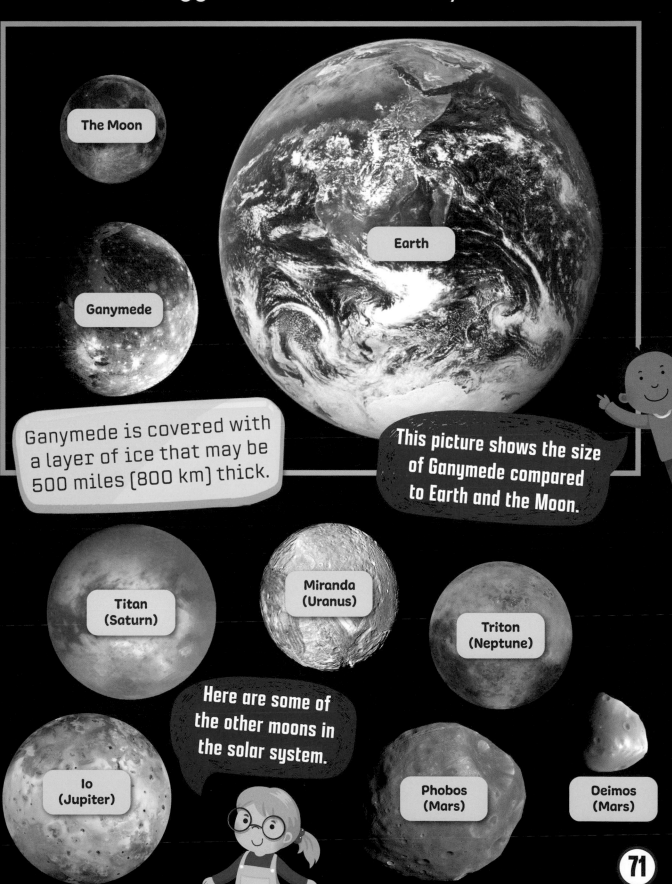

The Moon

Earth

Ganymede

Ganymede is covered with a layer of ice that may be 500 miles (800 km) thick.

This picture shows the size of Ganymede compared to Earth and the Moon.

Titan (Saturn)

Miranda (Uranus)

Triton (Neptune)

Here are some of the other moons in the solar system.

Io (Jupiter)

Phobos (Mars)

Deimos (Mars)

What Is an Asteroid?

An asteroid is a large space object made of rock mixed with metal.

Asteroids fly through space.

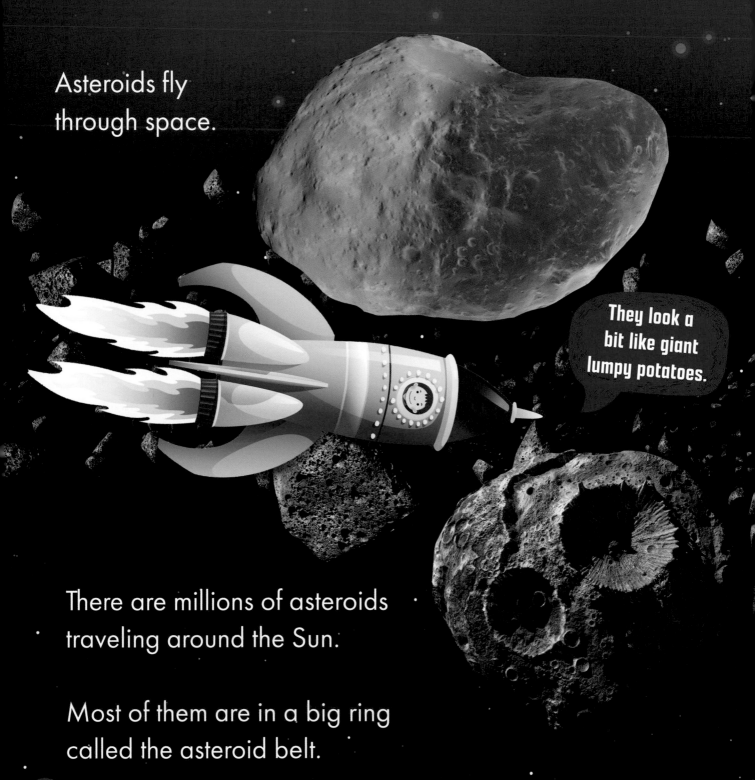

They look a bit like giant lumpy potatoes.

There are millions of asteroids traveling around the Sun.

Most of them are in a big ring called the asteroid belt.

The Asteroid Belt

- Jupiter
- Mars
- Mercury
- Sun
- Earth
- Venus
- Comet
- Asteroid belt

The biggest asteroid in the asteroid belt is called Ceres. It measures about 585 miles (940 km) across!

Ceres

Ceres is also a dwarf planet.

What Is a Comet?

A comet is like a giant space snowball.
It may be as big as a small town!

Tail

Comet

A comet is made of ice
mixed with rock and dust.

A comet's tail
may be millions of
miles long!

A comet travels around the Sun in an egg-shape.

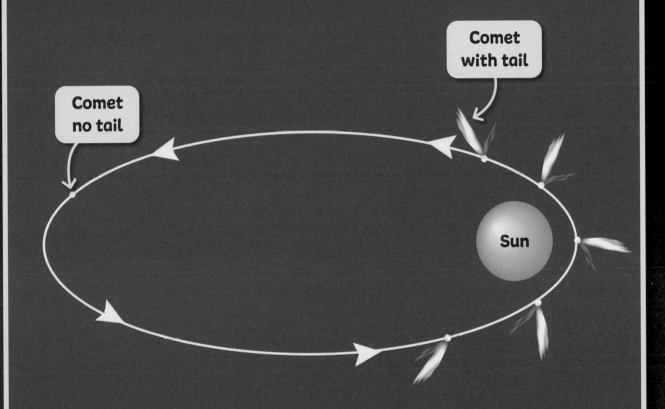

When it gets close to the Sun, a comet gets a long tail of gases and dust.

What Are Meteors and Meteorites?

Rocky chunks called meteoroids break off from asteroids and comets.

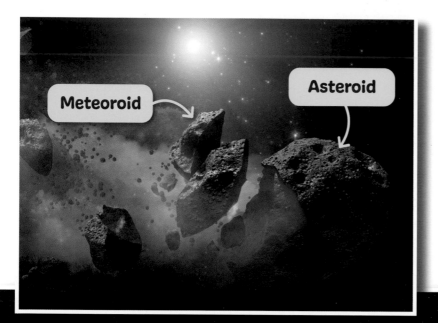

Meteoroid

Asteroid

Sometimes they fly toward Earth.

When they hit the gases around our planet, they burn up.

Meteors

This makes bright lights in the sky called meteors.

A meteor is also called a shooting star.

Sometimes a meteoroid doesn't burn up,
and it lands on Earth.

Then it is called a meteorite.

A large meteorite

A small meteorite

Could a Big Asteroid Hit Earth?

Asteroids and comets sometimes hit planets and moons.

They make big craters in the ground.

A large space object hit Earth about 50,000 years ago.

The crater is in Arizona.

The space object made this giant crater. More than 150 football fields could fit inside!

Crater

But don't worry!

Astronomers keep watch on space using telescopes and computers.

They are sure that none of the big space objects they can see will hit our planet.

How Do We Know So Much About Space?

Space scientists look at the universe with telescopes.

They also build spacecraft called **space probes** that fly to faraway places.

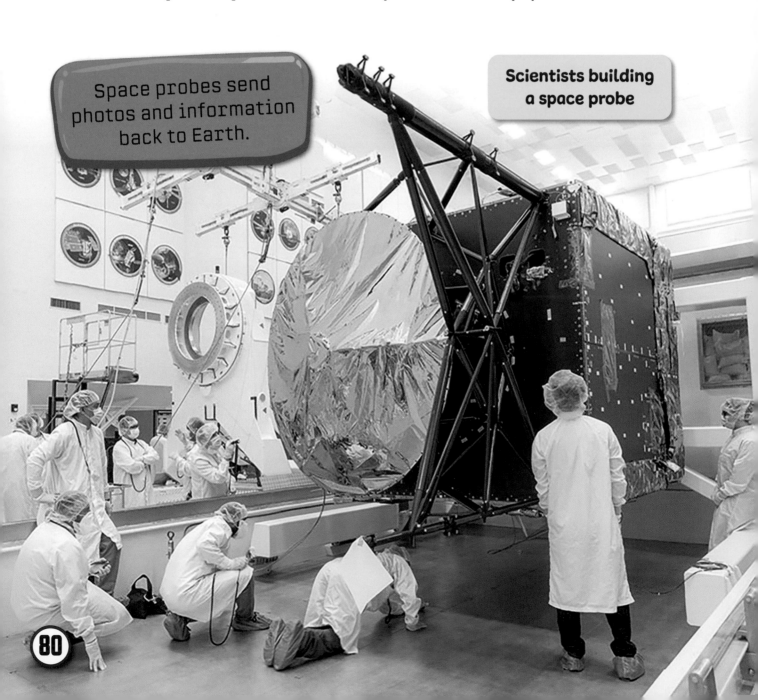

Space probes send photos and information back to Earth.

Scientists building a space probe

Juno

A space probe called *Juno* looked into Jupiter's clouds.

Cassini

A probe called *Cassini* flew into Saturn's icy, rocky rings.

A robot space probe called *OSIRIS-REx* landed on an asteroid.

Asteroid

OSIRIS-REx

OSIRIS-REx collected rock from the asteroid. It will bring the rock back to Earth in 2023.

Could I Be an Astronaut?

It takes six years to train to be an astronaut.

Astronauts learn how to fly a spacecraft.

Inside a simulator

They practice in a pretend spacecraft called a simulator.

It's a bit like playing a very difficult video game.

Astronaut Skills

- Be fit and healthy
- Be good at math and science
- Be brave at scary times
- Have a good memory

Astronauts practice being in space, where you feel weightless.

WOW! It's fun to float around.

Tim Peake

Yuri Malenchenko

Tim Kopra

Astronauts ready to go into space.

What is the International Space Station?

The International Space Station (ISS) is a place for living and working in space.

The space station is 250 miles (400 km) above Earth. It orbits around our planet 16 times each day.

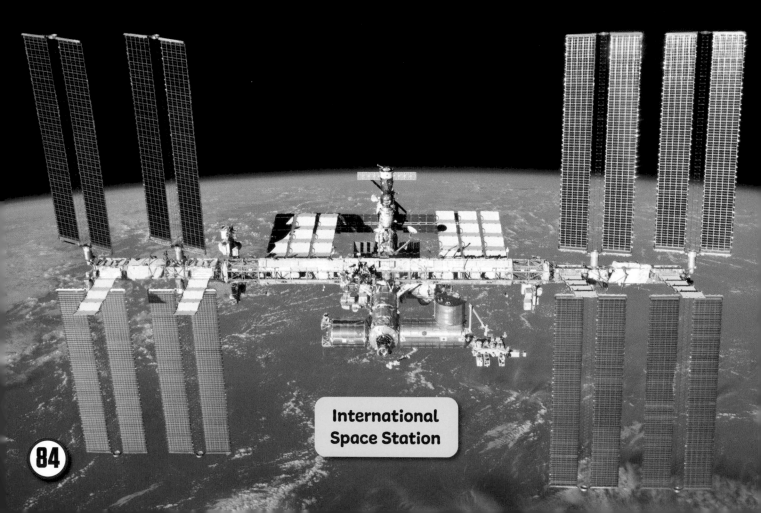

International Space Station

Astronauts live in some parts of the space station.

They do science work in other parts.

An astronaut in her sleeping bag bed

Growing plants in space

Earth

Sometimes astronauts do a spacewalk outside to fix the space station.

What Do Astronauts Eat on the Space Station?

The astronauts on the ISS only get a food delivery every few months.

Spinach

Crackers

Cookies

Candy

Their food must last for a long time.

Nuts

Beef

It comes tightly sealed in plastic bags.

Astronauts call this a space cheeseburger.

Tortilla

Tomato paste

Cheese

Beef

When a spacecraft brings supplies,
astronauts get fresh fruit and vegetables.

To save water on the ISS, the
astronauts' pee is collected. Then
it is cleaned and made back into
drinking water.

These astronauts
are drinking
recycled pee!

Why Is Our Planet Special?

Earth has rivers, lakes, and giant oceans.

No other planet in the solar system has water like this.

Trees and other plants grow here.

Animals and people live on Earth, too.

And all of them need water to survive.

Earth is the only planet we know of that has living things!

Is There Another Planet Like Earth?

There is no other planet like Earth in our solar system.

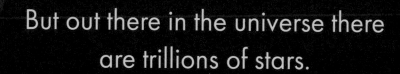

But out there in the universe there are trillions of stars.

Each one may have planets traveling around it.

This means there could be

trillions and **trillions** of planets

out there in space.

Scientists are looking for them with powerful telescopes.

Will we one day find another planet like Earth?

No one can say for sure!

Could There Be Aliens Out in Space?

Many scientists think that far from our solar system there may be other planets with living things.

Maybe tiny microbes will live there.

Perhaps these planets will have plants.

They may be home
to strange animals.

There might
even be aliens
living there!

Would you like to meet an alien?

My Space Words

asteroid
A large space rock that's orbiting, or traveling, around the Sun.

astronomer
A scientist who studies planets, moons, stars, and other objects in space.

comet
A space object made of ice, rock, and dust that is orbiting, or traveling, around the Sun.

crater
A large bowl-shaped hole in the ground.

dwarf planet
A ball-shaped object in space that is orbiting, or traveling, around the Sun. A dwarf planet is much smaller than the eight big, main planets.

eclipse
The blocking of the light from one space object by another.

microbe
A living thing that can only be seen with a microscope. Germs are a type of microbe.

moon
A round space object that orbits, or travels, around a planet.

nebula
A giant cloud of dust and gases in space where stars are made.

orbit
To circle, or travel around, another object.

planet
A large, ball-shaped object in space that is orbiting, or traveling, around a star.

telescope
A piece of equipment or a large machine used for looking into space.

solar system
The Sun and all the space objects that orbit, or travel around, the Sun.

universe
Everything that is in space, including Earth, the Sun, and other stars, planets, and moons.

space probe
A spacecraft that does not have any people on board. It is controlled by scientists on Earth.

volcano
An opening in the ground of a planet or moon that lets material from underground escape onto the surface. Often, super-hot, melted rock called lava bursts from a volcano.

star
A huge ball of burning gases in space. Our Sun is a star.

Big Space Quiz

1: What is a nebula?
 a) A giant cloud where stars form
 b) A big, lumpy space rock
 c) A type of alien

2: What is the Moon made of?
 a) Water and gases
 b) Cheese
 c) Rock

3: What is the Sun?
 a) A big, burning planet
 b) A star
 c) A type of space probe

4: Why is Earth a special planet?
 a) It is the biggest planet
 b) It has water, plants, animals, and people
 c) It is closest to the Sun

5: Which planet has robot explorers on it?
 a) Mars
 b) Uranus
 c) Jupiter

6: What is a comet?
 a) A giant gassy planet
 b) A giant space snowball
 c) One of Santa's reindeer

7: How many planets are there in the solar system?
 a) 82
 b) Trillions
 c) 8

8: How many astronauts have walked on the Moon?
 a) 2
 b) 12
 c) Only robots have visited the Moon

9: Which planet is the biggest in the solar system?
 a) Jupiter
 b) Mercury
 c) Neptune

10: What is Pluto?
 a) The biggest planet in the solar system
 b) A giant star
 c) A dwarf planet

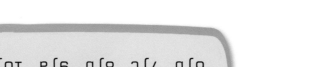

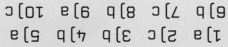

Answers:
1)a 2)c 3)b 4)b 5)a
6)b 7)c 8)b 9)a 10)c